Never Run at
Your Giant
with Your
Mouth Shut

Never Run at Your Giant with Your Mouth Shut

Unless otherwise indicated, all scriptural quotations are from the King James Version of the Bible.

Scripture taken from The Amplified Bible, Old Testament copyright 1965, 1987, by the Zondervan Corporation. The Amplified New Testament copyright 1958, 1987 by the Lockman Foundation. Used by permission.

Scripture taken from The Message. Copyright by Eugene H. Peterson, 1993, 1994, 1995. Used by permission of NavPress Publishing Group.

Scripture also taken from:
New English Bible. Copyright by Oxford University Press, 1961.
Revised Standard Version. Copyright by Thomas Nelson and Sons, 1952.
The Bible in Basic English. Copyright by University Press, 1965.
The Emphasized Bible. Copyright by J.B. Rotherham, 1976.
The Holy Bible, The New Berkeley Version. Copyright by Zondervan Publishing House.
The Jerusalem Bible. Copyright by Double Day and Company, Inc., 1968.
Weymouth's New Testament in Modern Speech. Copyright by James Clark and Company, 1909.

Quotations of F.F. Bosworth are taken from Christ the Healer (Grand Rapids, Michigan, Fleming H. Revell, 1973), p.80.

Some quotations are the author's paraphrase.

Never Run at Your Giant With Your Mouth Shut!
ISBN 978-1-889981-56-7

Published by MHM Publications
P.O. Box 12863
Alexandria, LA 71315

Copyright 2001 by Mark Hankins
All rights reserved.

TABLE OF CONTENTS

Faith is released by speaking. If you are silent, you lose by default!

1

WINNING THE WAR ON WORDS

"Never run at your giant with your mouth shut!" These are the words the Lord spoke to me as a key to killing my giants. We all face many giants in life that must be conquered before we can receive and do all that God has for us. As you know, some of these giants can be persistent. Speaking the Word of God releases God's power to win in each conflict. Winning the war of words is necessary to win the fight of faith. First Samuel 17 gives us a picture of the faith-filled words that were spoken and determined the outcome of the battle. As you can see from the following passage, David's word-war did not begin with Goliath; it actually began with Saul. You could call this the pre-fight warm up. Some people lose before they ever get to the real fight. Let's see how David won:

> *And David said to Saul, Let no man's heart fail because of him; thy servant will go and fight with this Philistine. And Saul said to David, Thou art not able to go against this Philistine to fight with him:*

for thou art but a youth, and he a man of war from his youth. And David said unto Saul, Thy servant kept his father's sheep, and there came a lion, and a bear, and took a lamb out of the flock: And I went out after him, and smote him, and delivered it out of his mouth: and when he arose against me, I caught him by his beard, and smote him and slew him. Thy servant slew both the lion and the bear: and this uncircumcised Philistine shall be as one of them, seeing he hath defied the armies of the living God. David said moreover, The

Lord that delivered me out of the paw of the lion, and out of the paw of the bear, he will deliver me out of the hand of this Philistine. And Saul said unto David, Go, and the Lord be with thee. And when the Philistine looked about, and saw David, he disdained him: for he was but a youth, and ruddy, and of a fair countenance. And the Philistine said unto David, Am I a dog, that thou comest to me with staves? And the Philistine cursed David by his gods. And the Philistine said to David, Come to me, and I will give thy flesh unto the fowls of the air, and to the beasts of the field. Then said David to the Philistine, Thou comest to me with a sword, and with a spear, and with a shield: but I come to thee in the name of the Lord of hosts, the God of the armies of Israel, whom thou hast defied. This day will the Lord deliver thee into mine hand; and I will smite thee, and take thine head from thee; and I will give the carcases of the host of the Philistines this day unto the fowls of the air, and to the wild beasts of the earth; that all the earth may know that there is a God in Israel.

And all this assembly shall know that the Lord saveth not with sword and spear: for the battle is the Lord's, and he will give you into our hands. And it came to pass, when the Philistine arose, and came and drew nigh to meet David, that David hasted, and ran toward the army to meet the Philistine. And David put his hand in his bag, and took thence a stone, and slang it, and smote the Philistine in his forehead, that the stone sunk into his forehead; and he fell upon his face to the earth. So David prevailed over the Philistine with a sling and with a stone, and smote the Philistine, and slew him; but there was no sword in the hand of David. Therefore David ran, and stood upon the Philistine, and took his sword, and drew it out of the sheath thereof, and slew him, and cut off his head there with. And when the Philistines saw their champion was dead, they fled.

- 1 Samuel 17:32-37, 42-51

This is the classic story of David and Goliath. The real battle was won before David actually killed Goliath. A war of words had to be won before victory could be consummated. The way the Lord said it to me was, "Never run at your giant with your mouth shut!"

Before David ran at Goliath a war of words went on.

Goliath said...
David said...
Goliath said...
David said...
David ran toward the Philistine...
David prevailed over the Philistine...

You know the story well. We all love it. I want to draw your attention to this part: David won the war of words before he won the victory.

Another example of winning is found in Matthew 4. Let's see how Jesus won the war of words with Satan.

And when the tempter came to him [Jesus], he said, If thou be the Son of God, command that these stones be made bread. But he answered and said, It is written, Man shall not live by bread alone, but by every word that proceedeth out of the mouth of God. Then the devil taketh him up into the holy city, and setteth him on a pinnacle of the temple, And saith unto him, If thou be the Son of

God, cast thyself down: for it is written, He shall give his angels charge concerning thee: and in their hands they shall bear thee up lest at any time thou dash thy foot against a stone. Jesus said unto him, It is written again, Thou shalt not tempt the Lord thy God. Again, the devil taketh him up into an exceeding high mountain, and showeth him all the kingdoms of the world, and the glory of them; And saith unto him, All these things will I give thee, if thou wilt fall down and worship me. And saith Jesus unto him, Get thee hence Satan: for it is written, Thou shalt worship the Lord thy God, and him only shalt thou serve. Then the devil leaveth him, and, behold angels came and ministered unto him.

- Matthew 4:3-11

In the same way, we see Jesus face Satan in the wilderness in Matthew 4. Jesus defeated Satan by speaking the Word of God.

Satan said…
Jesus said…
Satan said…
Jesus said…
Satan said…
Jesus said…

Notice that the Lord Jesus Christ won the war of words and put the devil on the run. Even Jesus had to "say" three times before the devil left. The power of speaking the Word of God is evident and necessary to win the fight of faith.

The spirit of faith believes and speaks (2 Corinthians 4:13). Jesus said in Mark 11:23, "Whosoever shall say...believe that those things which he saith...he shall have whatsoever he saith." In that verse Jesus clearly tells us how faith works. He said "believe" once. He said "say, saith, saith" three times. Faith is released by speaking. If you are silent, you lose by default. You must win the war of words to win in every conflict.

PRISONERS OF WORDS

A war of words is going on in each of our lives every day. Winning that war will determine life or death, blessing or cursing. Many people are held hostage by their words; they are prisoners of words. Proverbs 6:2 says, "Thou art snared with the words of thy mouth, thou art taken with the words of thy mouth." The *Jerusalem Bible* says, "...through words of yours you have been entrapped." *Basic English* says, "...the sayings of your lips have overcome you." According to Proverbs 18:21, "Death and life are in the power of the tongue."

James 3 tells us that the direction and destiny of our life is determined by the tongue.

We must win the war of words before we win in any area of life. God has supplied the ammunition and the Word power to win in every area. There is life, healing, joy, victory, and blessing in the Word of God. You are a believer. You must speak what you believe for victory to be yours.

The confession of your lips that has grown out of faith in your heart will absolutely defeat the adversary in every combat. That means Satan cannot win if you will hold fast to your confession and allow your words to register on your spirit.

GOD'S WORD IN YOUR MOUTH

You can see why the devil would fight you getting the Word in your mouth. Everything Jesus did is activated when you get the Word in your mouth and in your heart. Reinhard Bonnke said the Lord told him, "My Word in your mouth is just as powerful as My Word in My mouth."[1]

The thing you need to focus on is getting the Word in your mouth. When you get the Word in your mouth, you have the answer. The answer is already in the Word!

You are not in any way trying to replace God. Instead, you are releasing God. You have that authority as a believer. There is so much power in this you can see why the devil would want to gain control of your mouth.

You have the same spirit of faith that David had, Paul had, and the Lord Jesus had. Fight the good fight of faith. Believe and speak. Say what God has done for you in the plan of redemption. Say what Jesus has done through His blood and the power of His resurrection. God's Word spoken through your lips wins in every conflict!

Your words custom design and specifically shape your future.

Your voice is your ticket out of Satan's dominion.

Your words can limit you or loose you.

2

THE SPEECH CENTER EXERCISES DOMINION

A leading neurosurgeon has said that the speech center in the brain exercises dominion over the whole central nervous system. He also stated that this is a recent discovery of medical science. He said that you can cause different parts of the body to respond with stimuli to corresponding parts of the human brain, but when the speech center is stimulated, the whole central nervous system responds.

This means that when anyone says, "I am weak," the speech center sends out the message to the whole body to prepare to be weak. This must be the reason that God said, "Let the weak say, I am strong" (Joel 3:10).

BY YOUR WORDS

For in many things we offend all. If any man offend not in word, the same is a perfect man, and able to bridle the whole body. - James 3:2

Actually, James 3 makes it clear that the tongue controls not only the whole body, but also the destiny and quality of our lives. I like the way this passage reads in the Message Bible:

If you could find someone whose speech was perfectly true, you'd have a perfect person, in perfect control of life. A bit in the mouth of a horse controls the whole horse. A small rudder on a huge ship in the hands of a skilled captain sets course in the face of the strongest wind. A word out of your mouth may seem of no account, but it can accomplish nearly everything — or destroy it!
- James 3:2-5

This may seem to be a new discovery in medical science, but the Bible has revealed this fact for thousands of years. Medical science is finally finding out what the Bible says has been true all along.

James 3 says the tongue will determine the direction and the destination of your life. Your tongue will also determine the quality of your life.

First Peter 3:10 says, "For he that will love life, and see good days, let him refrain his tongue from evil, and his lips that they speak no guile."

You go to a doctor when something is wrong. The first thing he does is look at your tongue. When you go to God when something is wrong, the first thing God says is, "Say Ahh. I see the problem. It is written all over your tongue."

The speech center is the dominion center for our lives. Our words will make us or break us. Our words dominate both our inward man and outward man. Our words determine the boundaries of our lives. Our words can limit us or loose us.

God gave Adam dominion in the beginning through the power of the spoken word, and that fact has never changed. The Lord Jesus, the Last Adam, said, "By thy words thou shalt be justified, and by thy words thou shalt be condemned" (Matthew 12:37). Jesus also gave us the classic revelation of how faith works in Mark 11:23, where He said, "Whosoever shall say...he shall have whatsoever he saith." This is a fact that few people take as seriously as the Bible emphasizes.

GOD TOUCHES YOUR MOUTH TO CHANGE YOUR WORLD

Anytime God wants to change someone's life, He always touches their mouth. Anytime God wants to change a city or nation, He always touches someone's mouth. God changes lives through mouth-to-mouth resuscitation! He puts His Words in our mouth to bring life, salvation, or healing.

God touched Isaiah's mouth with a coal of fire and sent him to speak words that would change a nation. Those words are still changing lives today — thousands of years later! God touched Jeremiah's mouth and changed his life and a nation. The list of people goes on and on, but the most important thing is that right now God is touching your mouth and changing your world.

MAN IS A "SPEAKING SPIRIT"

And the Lord God formed man of the dust of the ground, and breathed into his nostrils the breath of life; and man became a living soul. - Genesis 2:7

A Hebrew scholar once said this verse could better be translated that man became "a speaking spirit." God created man in His own image with the capacity to speak and communicate. The power of speech was a major distinguishing factor between man and the animal kingdom.

Man was made "a speaking spirit" and given dominion. Satan also recognizes the power of spoken words and is constantly trying to get man to speak words that contaminate, defile, and destroy. A constant war is going on for "air time." Satan wants to stop the spoken Word of God in your personal life as well as in your city or nation.

YOUR VOICE IS YOUR TICKET OUT OF SATAN'S DOMINION

Say unto them, As truly as I live, saith the Lord, as you have spoken in mine ears, so will I do to you.
- Numbers 14:28

The story of the nation of Israel's failure to possess the Promised Land is clearly described in Numbers 13 and 14. Everyone in these two chapters got exactly what he said. Joshua and Caleb won the war of words when they said, "We are well able to possess the land." The other leaders said, "We are not able," and they died in the wilderness. Again, we can see the truth that God said, "I will do to you exactly as you said." Words are your "address" in the spirit realm. Words are the "mail" you send out — mail that is returned to you. Your words custom design and specifically shape your own future. Your voice is your ticket out of Satan's dominion. Your speech center exercises dominion in your life.

YOU HAVE BEEN FRAMED

"I have been framed." You often hear those words when working with prison inmates. Many times the person speaking doesn't realize how true those words really are. The truth is, everyone has been framed. Our words and the words of others have framed our world.

Hebrews 11:3 says that in the beginning God "framed" the worlds with His words. Everything we can see was framed with an unseen substance called faith. Faith is always made up of the spoken Word of God. Everything we can see was made out of words. The devil has gotten into people's lives and framed a false picture that is not in God's plan.

F.F. Bosworth said, "It is impossible to boldly claim by faith a blessing that you are not sure God is offering." You cannot boldly possess things that you don't understand are available to you. If your confession is wrong, your thinking is wrong, and you do without.

As we speak the Word of God, it tears down, roots out, builds, and plants (Jeremiah 1: 4-12). God wants us to speak His Words and frame the picture He has for us. He has a custom plan for each of us in Christ Jesus. Ephesians 2:10 says, "For we are his workmanship, created in

Christ Jesus unto good works, which God has before ordained that we should walk in them."

"LEGO" BIBLE BUILDING BLOCKS

Jesus said in Mark 11:23, "Whosoever shall say...believe those things which he saith...he shall have whatsoever he saith." He said "believe" once. He said "say, saith, saith" three times. Rev. Kenneth E. Hagin said the Lord told him he would have to do three times more teaching on the saying part than on the believing part, or people wouldn't get it. The speaking part is vital to faith. Faith is released or put to work by speaking. Again, if you are silent, you lose by default.

Jesus used three different Greek words for the speaking part of faith in Mark 11:23. "Whosoever shall say...believe that those things which he saith...he shall have whatsoever he saith."

The first word "say" is the Greek word *epo*, which means to command. It shows the authority of the believer.

The second word Jesus used is *laleo*, which means to speak out. Use your own voice! Be bold!

The third Greek word is *lego*. It means a systematic set discourse. At toy stores we see Lego® sets that contain building blocks for children to construct according to the diagram or picture on the box.

In Mark 11:22 Jesus instructs, "Have faith in God." He then gives us clear instructions on how faith works in Mark 11:23. He began the instructions this way, "For verily I say unto you...." This word "say" in Mark 11:23 is the Greek word *lego*. Jesus was constructing and giving us the building blocks to teach us how the believer's faith works.

Jesus said, "I am giving you the lego set of building blocks that you can use to frame your world according to the picture and diagram I have given you in the Word of God." Actually, Jesus began by giving us a lego, or a way to construct our world, "For verily I say unto you...."

The Bible has given us a lego

set of building blocks for salvation, healing, blessing, prosperity, and victory in life. Take the Word of God and build. Work together with God by putting His Word in your mouth and framing your future. It is not all up to God. You must do your part. Use your faith every day to frame your world. Your speech center exercises dominion in your life.

Your success and usefulness in this world will be measured by your confession and your tenacity to hold fast to that confession. In other words, don't just speak the confession; you must be tenacious as well.

God can be no bigger in you than you can confess Him to be. A spiritual law that few people recognize is that your words and your confessions actually shape and determine who you are and what you will become.

When I was 17 years old, I got a hold of Mark 11:23:

Whosoever shall say unto this mountain, Be removed, and be cast into the sea, and shall not doubt in his heart but shall believe that those things which he saith shall come to pass, he shall have whatsoever he saith.

I decided to stop saying what I had and to start having what I say.

Jesus has fought the battle for us and won.

Our identificaton with Him demands the identical confession of faith.

We must say the same thing that God says about us in Christ.

3

CONFESS UP

...Attentively consider the Apostle and High Priest of our confession – Jesus.
- Hebrews 3:1; Rotherham

...Inasmuch then as we have a great High Priest Who has [already] ascended and passed through the heavens, Jesus the Son of God, let us hold fast our confession [of faith in Him].
- Hebrews 4:14; Amplified

Using the word "confession" in our society conjures up the thought of someone admitting to something negative. When a person is trying to get someone else to confess or admit to something negative, they will use the expression "own up" or admit it. Sometimes a shorter version is used: "Fess up."

First John 1:9 speaks of the confession of sin or failure to the Lord for the restoration of fellowship; however, the New Testament has much more to say about confession in a positive light than in a negative light. Many believers today need to recognize the power of positive confession. In other words, they need to "own up" to the reality of all that Jesus has done and is doing for them. They need to "own up" to the reality of redemption and who they are in Christ.

You need to spend some time every day owning up to who Jesus is and who you are in Him. We should all fess up to the power of the blood of Jesus and that in Him we are redeemed, forgiven, healed, and blessed. It is necessary for us to own up to our redemption.

CONFESSION PRECEDES POSSESSION

Nothing will establish you and build your faith as quickly as the confession of who you are and what you have in Christ.

Confession precedes possession. Confession is the beginning of possession. Confession is owning up. Jesus is the Apostle and High Priest of our confession. He represents and responds to our words. He needs us to hold fast to our confession of faith in Him. He is waiting for us to say something that agrees with all He has done. He literally needs us to say something in faith that activates His work and power.

Your identification with Christ is activated by the identical confession of your mouth that "I am who God says I am. I have what God says I have. I can do what God says I can do." We must say the same thing that God says about us in Christ. If you are not impressed with who you are in Christ, you simply have not seen Him lately. He is glorified and all-powerful, and you are in Him. You must own up to it!

The Greek word translated "profession" or "confession" in the New Testament means *to say the same thing.* The power of positive confession means *to say the same thing* that the Word of God says about your situation. This is such a powerful truth because it is the way we are saved.

We are saved when we believe in our heart and confess

with our mouth that Jesus is Lord. Romans 10:9,10 says, "…For with the heart we believe unto righteousness and with the mouth confession is made unto salvation." Confession is owning up to the Lordship of Jesus and to all that salvation includes. Powerful words that come from the believer's mouth recreate the human spirit and impart eternal life to a person.

F. F. Bosworth said, "A spiritual law that few recognize is that our confession rules us. It is what we confess with our lips that really dominates our inner being. Nothing will establish you and build your faith as quickly as confession. The confession of your lips that has grown out of faith in your heart will absolutely defeat the adversary in every combat. God can be no bigger in you than you confess Him to be."[2]

Sometimes people trying to be humble are just being ignorant. Yes, we should humble ourselves under the mighty hand of God that He may exalt us in due time. However, there are things that are timely and things that are timeless. There are things that require the right season, and there are things concerning your redemption that are "open season" all year. God is always ready to save, heal, deliver, and bless. Jesus has already passed through the heavens; He is now watching over and waiting for your confession. It is now open season and all things are possible!

> *Fight the good fight of faith, lay hold on eternal life, whereunto thou art also called, and hast professed a good profession among many witnesses.*
> *- 1 Timothy 6:12*

The Holy Spirit said this through the Apostle Paul. The good fight of faith requires a good confession. The fight of faith is not a losing fight; it is a winning fight. The winning fight requires a winning confession. Jesus has fought the battle for us and won. Our identification with Him demands the identical confession of faith. We win by saying the same thing. The spirit of faith declares the outcome in the middle of adversity. We hold fast to our confession. We can see the end from the beginning of trouble. We consider Jesus and fix our eyes and our confession on Him.

Own up to your victory in Christ Jesus. Say, "Now thanks be unto God who always causeth us to triumph in Christ," (2 Corinthians 2:14).

Settle for nothing less than 100 percent victory. It is yours now. Confess up! Own up! Fess up! Admit it! You are a new creature in

Christ. You are the righteousness of God in Him. Say now, "In Christ, I am blessed."

> *That the communication*
> *of thy faith may become*
> *effectual by the*
> *acknowledging of every*
> *good thing that is in you in*
> *Christ Jesus.*
> *- Philemon 6*

> *...full recognition and*
> *appreciation and*
> *understanding and precise*
> *knowledge of every good*
> *thing that is ours in (our*
> *identification with) Christ*
> *Jesus. - Amplified*

For our faith to become fully effective, we must continually acknowledge every good thing that is in us in Christ. Sometimes our faith is like an automobile engine that has eight cylinders, but is only working on five or six. There is much more power available when we are working on all eight cylinders. Sometimes we are putting along — choking — because we are not acknowledging every good thing in us in Christ.

There is a wealth of good things in you in Christ. They are not just in Christ; they are in you because you are in Christ. More than 130 scriptures in the New Testament use the phrase, "in Christ," "in

Him," and "in Whom." Every time you see those two words, underline them and say, "That's who I am, and that's what I have." 2 Corinthians 5:17, 2 Corinthians 5:21, and 1 Corinthians 1:30 are a good start!

FITTED TO YOUR LIPS

For it is a pleasant thing if thou keep them within thee; they shall withal be fitted in thy lips. That thy trust may be in the Lord....
- Proverbs 22:18, 19

The Word of God is custom fitted for your lips. The Word of God was made to be spoken.

Confession is fundamental to faith. E.W. Kenyon said, "Confession builds the road over which faith carries its mighty cargo."[3] *The Amplified Bible* translates Proverbs 22:18 this way: "For it will be pleasant if you keep them in your mind [believing them]; your lips will be accustomed to [confessing] them." I like that. Your lips should be accustomed to confessing the Word of God. The Word is custom or tailor made for your mouth and your situation.

The Word of God was spoken before it was written and it was written so it could be spoken. Jesus is the Apostle and High Priest of your confession. "Whosoever shall say…he shall have whatsoever he saith…" (Mark 11:23).

Jesus is literally waiting for you to confess. As we saw, the word "confess" literally means *to say the same thing.* In other words, He has already said something about you, but He needs you to say the same thing.

Every benefit and blessing that is in us in Christ must be acknowledged and declared. For salvation to work for you, it must be in your mouth. For prosperity to work for you, it must be in your mouth. Say, "I am blessed coming in and going out. I am the head and not the tail, above and not beneath" (Galatians 3:13; Deuteronomy 28).

For healing to work for you, it must be in your mouth. Say, "…

by his stripes I am healed" (1 Peter 2:24). The Word will heal you if you will continually confess it! Say what God says about you. There is healing in the Word.

AN EXPLOSION OF POWER

And they overcame him [Satan] by the blood of the Lamb, and by the word of their testimony....
- Revelation 12:11

The tremendous power in the blood of Jesus is activated by adding your testimony to it. Your confession, testimony, and declaration of the blood of Jesus put the devil on the run. Satan, the accuser of the brethren, is constantly accusing us. The blood of Jesus when mixed with faith always overcomes the enemy. Romans 3:25 says, "...through faith in His blood."

Mixing faith with the blood of Jesus is like mixing nitro with glycerin. There is always an explosion of power! Our lips should be accustomed to confessing the power of the blood of Jesus and all that has been purchased for us in Him.

Make a personal daily list of scriptures that acknowledge who you are, what you have, and what you can do because you are in Christ (see Chapter 6).

Own up to what God has made you in Christ. God is always right and confession is agreeing with God and His Word. Every time you speak the Word, agree saying, "I agree with God." Say it now: "Christ hath redeemed me from the curse of the law. I am redeemed."

Say it to yourself quietly when you can. Talk to yourself. Say it out loud when it's appropriate. Then repeat it over and over again. There is a fight to faith but it's a good fight because it's one you win.

Next, say it until your whole being swings into harmony and into line with the Word of God. In other words, say it until your spirit starts lining up with the words you speak. They register on your heart and on your mind. You start seeing yourself healed and blessed.

As you hold fast to your confession of faith, you will find that your faith will advance and be more effective. Confess up! Never run at your giant with your mouth shut!

The Word of God spoken to us must be spoken through us.

4

WORDS

Who shall tell thee words, whereby thou and all thy house shall be saved. And as I began to speak, the Holy Ghost fell on them, as on us at the beginning.
- Acts 11:14, 15

Here the Apostle Peter was telling the leaders of the church at Jerusalem about his unusual experience at a Gentile's house.

He was quoting Cornelius' experience with the angel who said, "Who shall tell thee words, whereby thou and all thy house shall be saved."

People are saved by hearing words. Words are carriers of salvation. Notice also how the Holy Ghost "fell on them" the same as in Acts 2. The account in Acts 10:44 says, "While Peter yet spake these words, the Holy Ghost fell on all them which heard the word."

Notice the Holy Ghost fell specifically where people heard the Word. The Spirit of God always lands on the Word. As we speak the Word of God, it opens heaven, and the Holy Spirit falls on us to bring the power of God in this world. These are words that bring salvation, deliverance, healing, blessing, and victory. These are words that move the Holy Spirit of God.

I AM COME FOR THY WORDS

The angel Gabriel, speaking to Daniel, said, "...I am come for thy words" (Daniel 10:12). Words move not only God and the Holy Spirit; angels respond to words. Here you see angels on assignment going to the place where the right words were spoken. Words of believing prayer and words of faith move heaven to work on Earth. How important it is for us to understand the power of the spoken word.

THE WELCOMING WORD TO GOD

The word of faith is not such a difficult thing. The Gospel is called the word of faith in Romans 10:8. The Word is near you. Salvation is near you. Healing is near you. Blessing is near you. How close? It is in your mouth and your heart.

The word that saves us is right here, as near as the tongue in your mouth, as close as the heart in your chest. It's the word of faith that welcomes God to go to work and set things right for us. This is the core of our preaching. Say the welcoming word to God — "Jesus is my Master" — embracing body and soul, God's work of doing in us what He did in raising Jesus from the dead. That's it. You're not "doing" anything; you're simply calling out to God, trusting him to do it for you. That's salvation. With your whole being you embrace God setting things right, and then you say it right out loud: "God has set everything right between him and me!

- Romans 10:8-10 (MSG)

"Say the welcoming word of faith." I like that. Acknowledge the Lord Jesus Christ and all He has done for you. Dare to open the door to the supernatural by believing and speaking. God wants to work for you; He just needs you to open the door. Say it out loud. Hold fast to your confession of faith. Win the war of words. God has given us all the ammunition we need. Some daily confessions of faith are found in Chapter 6.

The Holy Spirit gives us God-breathed words that we can speak again and again to help us win.

Putting God's Word in our mouth gives us mouth-to-mouth resuscitation from God.

5

INSPIRED UTTERANCE

As powerful as the written Word of God is, the prophetic word given under the inspiration of the Holy Spirit is also just as powerful. Prophecy is inspired utterance. The simple gift of prophecy is for exhortation, edification, and comfort. Every Spirit-filled believer can and should prophesy. This kind of inspired utterance is a word in season to those who are weary or are facing a challenge.

The Lord God hath given me the tongue of the learned, that I should know how to speak a word in season to him that is weary: he wakeneth morning by morning, he wakeneth mine ear to hear as the learned.
- Isaiah 50:4

FIGHTING WORDS TO WIN THE WAR

This charge I commit unto thee, son Timothy, according to the prophecies which went before on thee, that thou by them mightest war a good warfare.
- 1 Timothy 1:18

The Apostle Paul was telling Timothy to remember the prophecies (inspired utterance) concerning him. You need to use such words to win the war concerning your future. Again, the Holy Spirit helps us win the war of words.

...in accordance with the prophetic utterances which pointed to you.
- Revised Standard Version

...so that you may with their aid put up a splendid fight.
- New Berkley Version

...that being equipped with them you may... - Weymouth

...that inspired by them you may wage the good warfare.
- Revised Standard Version

MOUTH-TO-MOUTH RESUSCITATION

The Holy Spirit gives us God-breathed Words that we can speak again and again to help us win. I call this "mouth-to-mouth" resuscitation. When we get words from God's mouth into our mouth, we breathe the life and ability of heaven into our lives. The Word of God was spoken before it was written, and it was written that it might be spoken.

...Man shall not live by bread alone, but by every word that proceedeth from the mouth of God.

- Matthew 4:4

Many times in my life the Holy Spirit has given me a prophetic word that has made the difference in a battle I was in. We can win every battle with the Word. Recently, the Holy Spirit gave this simple prophetic word to my wife, Trina. It is a word in season.

God is on my side,
For the blood has been applied.

Every need shall be
supplied,
Nothing shall be denied.
So I enter into rest,
And know that I am
blessed.
I have passed the test,
I will get God's best!

We have used these prophetic words along with many others to win many battles. The Word of God in our mouth puts the devil on the run. The ammunition is being delivered, so just load up and fire by speaking the Word.

And He hath made my
mouth like a sharp sword;
in the shadow of his hand

hath he hid me, and made me a polished shaft; in his quiver hath he hid me.
- Isaiah 49:2

He made my tongue his sharp sword....
- New English Bible

The sword of the Spirit is the Word of God. What a weapon we have in our mouth. When we believe and speak, mountains must move. We have authority as believers. We must win the war of words to win the fight of faith. One general said that in every battle there is a 10-minute span of time that is so crucial, it determines the outcome of the battle. Ten minutes can determine whether you win or lose.

The biggest battle takes place right in our own mouth. Our tongue will determine the outcome of life or death, blessing or cursing, winning or losing. Let's take the written Word of God and the inspired utterances of the Holy Spirit, speak with boldness, and win the war of words. When you run at your giant, speak the Word of God!

*I am what God says
I am.*

*I have what God says
I have.*

*I can do what God
says I can do.*

6

DAILY CONFESSIONS OF FAITH

Make these confessions daily and watch your faith grow.

I believe in my heart that God raised Jesus from the dead, and I confess with my mouth that Jesus Christ is Lord. Jesus is my Lord. (Romans 10:9, 10)

I have been born again. God is my very own Father, and I am His very own child. (Romans 8:14, 15)

I am a new creature in Christ Jesus. Old things are passed away; behold, all things are new. (2 Corinthians 5:17)

I can do all things through Christ who strengthens me. (Philippians 4:13)

I know I have eternal life. The very life and nature of God is in me. (1 John 5:11, 12)

By the blood of Jesus, I overcome all the works of the devil. (Revelation 12:11)

Greater is He that is in me than He that is in the world. (1 John 4:4)

Jesus said He would never leave me nor forsake me, so I can boldly say, "The Lord is my Helper, I will not fear what man can do unto me." (Hebrews 13:5)

It is God who works in me both to will and to do of His good pleasure. (Philippians 2:13)

I have been made the righteousness of God in Christ Jesus. (2 Corinthians 5:21)

My God supplies all my need according to His riches in glory by Christ Jesus. (Philippians 4:19)

The Lord is my shepherd. I shall not want or lack for anything. (Psalm 23:1)

The Lord is the strength of my life. I am strong in the Lord. (Psalm 27:1)

ENDNOTE

Chapter 1

1. Ron Steele, Plundering Hell to Populate Heaven: The Reinhard Bonnke Story (Tulsa, Oklahoma: Albury Press, 1987), p. 47.

Chapter 3

2. F.F. Bosworth, Christ the Healer (Grand Rapids, Michigan: Fleming H. Revel/Baker Book House Company, 1973), pp. 143, 146, 147.

3. Don Gossett and E.W. Kenyon, The Power of Your Words (Blaine, Washington, Don and Joyce Gossett, 1977), p. 32.

ACKNOWLEDGMENTS

Special Thanks to my wife, Trina.

My son, Aaron and his wife, Errin Cody; their daughters, Avery Jane and Macy Claire, their son, Jude Aaron.

My daughter, Alicia and her husband, Caleb; their sons, Jaiden Mark, Gavin Luke, Landon James, and Dylan Paul, their daughter Hadley Marie.

My parents, Pastor B.B. and Velma Hankins, who are now in Heaven with the Lord.

My wife's parents, Rev. William and Ginger Behrman.

ABOUT THE AUTHORS

Mark and Trina Hankins travel nationally and internationally preaching the Word of God with the power of the Holy Spirit. Their message centers on the spirit of faith, who the believer is in Christ, and the work of the Holy Spirit.

After over forty years of pastoral and traveling ministry, Mark and Trina are now ministering full-time in campmeetings, leadership conferences, and church services around the world and across the United States.

Mark and Trina have written several books. For more information on Mark Hankins Ministries, log on to the website, www.markhankins.org.

MARK HANKINS MINISTRIES PUBLICATIONS

SPIRIT-FILLED SCRIPTURE STUDY GUIDE
A comprehensive study of scriptures in over 120 different translations on topics such as: Redemption, Faith, Finances, Prayer and many more.

THE BLOODLINE OF A CHAMPION - THE POWER OF THE BLOOD OF JESUS
The blood of Jesus is the liquid language of love that flows from the heart of God and gives us hope in all circumstances. In this book, you will clearly see what the blood has done FOR US but also what the blood has done IN US as believers.

TAKING YOUR PLACE IN CHRIST
Many Christians talk about what they are trying to be and what they are going to be. This book is about who you are NOW as believers in Christ.

PAUL'S SYSTEM OF TRUTH
Paul's System of Truth reveals man's redemption in Christ, the reality of what happened from the cross to the throne and how it is applied for victory in life through Jesus Christ.

THE SECRET POWER OF JOY
If you only knew what happens in the Spirit when you rejoice, you would rejoice everyday. Joy is one of the great secrets of faith. This book will show you the importance of the joy of the Lord in a believer's life.

11:23 – THE LANGUAGE OF FAITH

Never under-estimate the power of one voice. Over 100 inspirational, mountain-moving quotes to "stir up" the spirit of faith in you.

LET THE GOOD TIMES ROLL

This book focuses on the five key factors to heaven on earth: The Holy Spirit, Glory, Faith, Joy, and Redemption. The Holy Spirit is a genius. If you will listen to Him, He will make you look smart.

THE POWER OF IDENTIFICATION WITH CHRIST

Learn how God identified us with Christ in His death, burial, resurrection, and seating in Heaven. The same identical life, victory, joy, and blessings that are In Christ are now in you. This is the glory and the mystery of Christianity – the power of the believer's identification with Christ.

REVOLUTIONARY REVELATION

This book provides excellent insight on how the spirit of wisdom and revelation is mandatory for believers to access their call, inheritance, and authority in Christ.

FAITH OPENS THE DOOR TO THE SUPERNATURAL

In this book you will learn how believing and speaking open the door to the supernatural.

THE SPIRIT OF FAITH

The Spirit of Faith is necessary to do the will of God and fulfill your divine destiny. Believing AND speaking are necessary ingredients in the spirit of faith. If you ONLY knew what was on the other side of your mountain, you would move it!

DIVINE APPROVAL: UNDERSTANDING RIGHTEOUSNESS

One of the most misunderstood subjects in the Bible is righteousness. The Gospel of Christ is a revelation of the righteousness of God, and the center of the Gospel reveals the righteousness of God. Understanding you have GOD'S DIVINE APPROVAL on your life sets you free from the sense of rejection, inadequacy or inferiority.

GOD'S HEALING WORD
by Trina Hankins

Trina's testimony and a practical guide to receiving healing through meditating on the Word of God. This guide includes: testimonies, practical teaching, Scriptures & confessions, and a CD with Scriptures & confessions (read by Mark Hankins).